Why
do people drink
Alcohol?

Julie Johnson

HODDER
Wayland

an imprint of Hodder Children's Books

© 2000 White-Thomson Publishing Ltd

Produced for Hodder Wayland by
White-Thomson Publishing Ltd
2/3 St Andrew's Place
Lewes
BN7 1UP
East Sussex

Other titles in this series:
Why do people take drugs?
Why do people gamble?
Why do people join gangs?
Why do people smoke?
Why do people live on the streets?

Series concept: Alex Woolf
Editor: Liz Gogerly
Consultant: John Bennett, Health Education
          Advisor, Birmingham
Picture Researcher: Gina Brown – Glass Onion
          Pictures
Cover Design: Hodder Children's Books
Inside Design: Mark Whitchurch Art & Design
Proofreader: Alison Cooper

Published in Great Britain in 2000 by Hodder
Wayland, an imprint of Hodder Children's Books

The right of Julie Johnson to be identified as the
author of this work has been asserted by them in
accordance with the Copyright, Designs and
Patents Act 1988.

A Catalogue record for this book is available from
the British Library.

ISBN 0 7502 2760 5

Printed and bound in Italy by G. Canale & C.S.p.A.

Hodder Children's Books
A division of Hodder Headline Limited
338 Euston Road
London
NW1 3BH

Picture acknowledgements
The publisher would like to thank the following
for their kind permission to use their pictures:
Allsport 45; UK Bridgeman Art Library 12; Camera
Press 22; Cephas (title page), 8, 41; Mary Evans 10;
Eye Ubiquitous/ Paul Seheult 42; Ronald Grant
Archives 31; Angela Hampton 14, 38; Robert
Harding 6 (bottom) 27, 30; Hodder Wayland
Picture Library 11 (top and bottom), 13, 40/
A. Haslon 16 (bottom)/ Gordon Clements 17/
Tizzie Knowles 20, 37/ Howard J Davies 28; Impact/
Alex MacNaughton 4, 23/ Steve Parry 9/ Andy
Johnstone 19, 25, 29, 44 / Bruce Stephens 36;
Panos 18/ Liba Taylor 5, 24/ Sean Sprague 7/ Mark
Schlossman 33/ Clive Shirley 35/ Giacomo Pirozzi
42; Popperfoto 26, 32, 39; Skyjold 16 (top); Tony
Stone (cover); Topham Picturepoint 34.

Contents

1. What is alcohol?

What do you think alcohol is?

▲ *Young women having a drink together after work – social drinking is part of life for many people.*

Do you take drugs? If you asked most people this question they would reply that they do not. However, if they take medicines, drink alcohol, smoke cigarettes or even drink tea or coffee they are drug users. These are all drugs or substances which affect the mind and body in some way.

A drug is something which when taken into our bodies changes the way our bodies work. Alcohol is a depressant drug because it causes our bodies to slow down and we lose our inhibitions. This could make someone slur their words but it could also make them more talkative.

FACT:
Alcohol is often not thought of as a drug - largely because its use is common for both religious and social purposes in most parts of the world. It is a drug, however, and compulsive drinking in excess is one of modern society's most serious problems.
Addiction Research Foundation, Toronto, Canada.

In most parts of the world, alcohol is a socially accepted drug. It is a legal drug, which is used by many people in lots of different places, for a variety of reasons. People may have a beer at a party, a glass of wine with a meal, or visit a pub or wine bar on their way home from work. Some people use alcohol to help them relax at the end of a busy day. Homeless people may drink alcohol to help them cope with having no job or home.

'I think that as long as you drink in moderation, alcohol is OK. It's when people go out and get drunk that the problems begin.'
Sophia, 16.

▼ *A group of Mexican men enjoy a beer together.*

How is alcohol made?

Alcohol is a chemical called ethyl alcohol or ethanol. Alcohol can be made from most kinds of food, including fruit, grain or vegetables. It is made through processes called fermentation and distillation. These processes produce an intoxicating drink, which can vary in strength, depending on how it is made. Ethanol is a clear liquid but different kinds of alcohol get their colour from the products which are added during or after fermentation.

Beer is usually made from hops or barley mixed with water. Yeast is then added and fermentation begins. Alcohol is slowly produced.

▼ *Spirits, such as whisky, are distilled in large factories like this one in the Trossachs in Scotland.*

Wine can be made from many things, for example, fruits, rice and vegetables such as potatoes and parsnips. The most widely drunk wine is made from grapes. The juice of the crushed grapes is mixed with yeast and left to ferment in a warm environment. Yeast gradually changes the sugar in the juice into alcohol.

Spirits (whisky, vodka, gin and rum) are also made from grains, fruit and vegetables. Whisky is made from malted barley. Vodka is made from wheat, rye or potatoes. Gin is usually made from rye or barley and then flavoured with juniper berries. Spirits are first fermented and then distilled to make the alcohol content stronger and purer. The spirit is then stored for between six months and several years to improve the taste.

▲ *These women are making beer, using a local recipe, in Tanzania, Africa.*

FACT:
Many different countries have their own traditional drink made from local produce. In Ireland people drink potcheen, which is a strong spirit made from potatoes. In Jamaica there is a local gin made from bananas.

Types of alcohol

There are many kinds of alcohol made throughout the world. These vary from region to region depending upon the ingredients available in that area. The main types of alcohol are:

- beer (includes lager, ale and stout)
- wine (includes white, rosé and red wine, and champagne)
- cider
- fortified wine (includes sherry, port and vermouth)
- spirits (includes whisky, gin, vodka, brandy and rum)
- liqueurs or flavoured spirits

Each type of alcoholic drink contains a different amount of pure alcohol. Beer and wine contain less alcohol than spirits or fortified wine. For example, beer contains about 3.5–5 per cent alcohol by volume, wine contains about 12 per cent alcohol by volume, fortified wines contain about 20 per cent alcohol by volume and spirits usually contain about 40 per cent alcohol by volume.

▼ *Different kinds of alcohol are lined up on a bar-counter. Some drinks are drunk neat while others have mixers added.*

case study · case study · case study · case study · case study

Jake's first experience of strong alcohol was when he was on holiday when he was fourteen years old. In the bars, the bar staff didn't ask people how old they were, and Jake and his friends were able to get any type of drink they wanted. Jake usually drank lager but decided to try spirits for the first time. After an hour, he began to feel dizzy and sick. Later he threw up all over his friend. He felt awful the next day and had a terrible hangover – one he'll never forget.

Some alcohol, such as wine, is usually drunk on its own. Other types of alcohol can be either drunk on their own or mixed with another drink. Sometimes, lemonade is added to lager or beer to make shandy. Spirits are stronger than other forms of alcohol and are usually mixed with a non-alcoholic drink called a mixer. Mixers, such as lemonade, orange juice, tonic water or soda, are added to the spirit and help to make it taste better and not as strong.

▶ *Most teenage boys drink lager and beer and experiment with spirits occasionally.*

2. Alcohol-past and present

Is alcohol something new?

People have been making and drinking alcohol for thousands of years. The earliest evidence of wine production is from almost 6,000 years ago in the Middle East. The ancient Egyptians made beer from grain as early as 2250 BC. In Scotland, pots containing traces of ale have been dated to about 2000 BC.

▲ Bacchus, the god of wine, was worshipped by the Romans. Festivals in his honour were often drunken occasions.

Some ancient peoples worshipped alcohol as a source of 'good'. The Romans had their own god of wine called Bacchus, and alcohol became an essential part of many Roman celebrations, social gatherings and rituals.

FACT:
In the early twentieth century, small amounts of alcohol were sometimes used by mothers to quieten restless babies. Up until the late twentieth century, mothers gave their babies gripe water, which contains alcohol. It was believed that gripe water would take away the discomfort of wind which babies have after feeding.

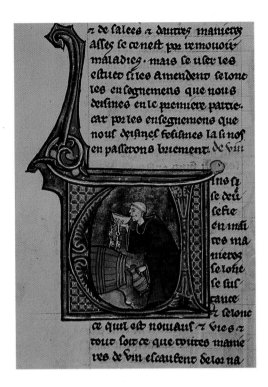

There are references to alcohol in the Bible. After the great flood, Noah planted a vineyard and began to produce wine. However, he did not always restrain his drinking and it is told how one day he got so drunk he collapsed.

Alcohol has been used down the centuries in a variety of ways. It has been used as a medicine for the seriously ill and has been given as a tonic for people who are run-down. For many years, wine was given to people to pep them up after a shock or illness. Spirits were even used as a painkiller before surgery. In Europe, it was often considered safer to drink ale rather than water which carried many diseases.

▲ *Monks have produced and drunk alcohol throughout their history. This monk is drinking ale.*

▼ *This picture from 1823 shows people collecting and pressing apples to make cider.*

Alcohol abuse down the ages

Throughout history, the use and misuse of alcohol has been condemned. As more and more breweries and distilleries produced greater amounts of alcoholic drinks, drunkenness became an increasing problem.

In Elizabethan England (1558–1603), people who consumed too much alcohol were put into a bottomless beer barrel known as a 'drunkard's cloak'. Holes were cut in the side of the barrel for the offender's arms and they were made to walk through the streets wearing the barrel.

▲ *This painting from the late eighteenth century shows the drunken behaviour of men in a London private club.*

By the eighteenth century, most countries had passed laws which attempted to regulate the use of alcohol. Licences had to be granted to taverns and inns that wished to trade in alcohol. However, the consumption of alcohol steadily rose, as did the concern about the misuse of alcohol.

The USA, Norway, Finland, Sweden and Canada, all of which were strongly Protestant countries, banned alcohol in the 1920s. The most famous of these campaigns against alcohol was started in 1920 in the USA and was called Prohibition. Prohibition aimed to stop the production and consumption of alcohol.

Despite over 300,000 convictions for illegal drinking in this period, people continued to find ways of making and drinking alcohol. Criminals, known as bootleggers, made money from the drinkers' illegal activities. As there was no quality control on the alcohol being produced and sold, many people died from drinking impure alcohol. In 1933, the American public grew so unhappy with the situation that they insisted that Prohibition was stopped.

> 'Prohibition makes you want to cry into your beer and denies you the beer to cry into.'
> *Don Marquis, archy and mehitabel, 1927.*

◀ *During the American Prohibition era people did strange things. This woman is wearing a special garment called a 'Rummy Apron' in which she could hide her drink.*

13

The law and alcohol

Laws about drinking alcohol vary a great deal all over the world. There are laws about the age at which young people are allowed to use or buy alcohol. Other laws include where and when people can drink, and the measures of each kind of alcohol that can be sold on licensed premises.

'Why do they make such strong drinks if they are dangerous? I think they should only let people at bars and pubs have a limited amount of alcohol.'
Joanna, 12, Glasgow, UK.

In the USA, most states have raised the minimum legal age for drinking alcohol from eighteen to twenty-one. In New Zealand and Japan, the minimum age is twenty. In Britain, the law gradually allows people more freedom to drink alcohol and at eighteen, they are also allowed to buy alcohol from most licensed premises. In France, the laws governing alcohol are not as strict as in other countries – the minimum age for drinking is fourteen to eighteen.

Despite the minimum legal age for drinking, under-age drinking is an increasing problem in most countries.

▲ *A British policeman*
does a breathalyser test on
a driver who has been
involved in a car accident.

Laws about alcohol, particularly about the minimum age for drinking, are often broken. One of the biggest problems is under-age drinking. In many cases it is difficult for bar staff or shopkeepers to tell how old somebody is – especially when somebody has purposely tried to look older than they are.

The laws about drinking and driving also vary from country to country. However, most countries have tried to crack down on drinking and driving with tight laws which aim to limit the amount people drink. Governments set a legal alcohol limit and penalties for breaking these limits include heavy fines, disqualification from drinking and even prison sentences.

Religion and alcohol

Each religion has its own views on drinking alcohol. Most religions tolerate moderate drinking. However, some religions forbid any alcohol consumption.

Many Christians believe that it is acceptable to drink alcohol responsibly and in moderation. But some Christian groups, such as Methodists and Pentecostals, encourage their members not to drink at all. However, wine is used in Christian religious ceremonies. Priests use wine in the Mass or Holy Communion service to represent the blood of Christ.

▲ *Wine is part of the Christian Mass or Holy Communion service.*

In the Jewish faith, moderate and responsible use of alcohol is accepted. Wine is used in many Jewish religious ceremonies. One of these is Shabbat, which is celebrated every Friday night.

◄ *This Jewish family raises a glass of wine during Shabbat.*

At the beginning of the meal everyone eats a piece of bread while the father raises a glass of wine and blesses it, saying, 'Blessed is the name of the Lord, King of the Universe, who has given us the fruit of the vine'. Then, everyone takes a sip of the wine.

In some Muslim countries, it is forbidden to drink alcohol or to have anything to do with people who produce and sell it. Strict Muslims will take great care not to come into any contact with alcohol. They should not even sell grapes to anyone who may make wine with them. To give or receive alcohol as a present is also forbidden. However, some Muslim countries, such as Turkey and the Lebanon, do produce wine.

Sikhs believe it is important to remember God in everything they think and do. They are encouraged to keep a clear mind, so, for this reason, many Sikhs do not drink alcohol.

> 'Keeping the body fit and healthy is part of serving God, for it is impossible to know and understand anything of the creator's will if one is ill. Therefore a person should avoid anything whatever that undermines bodily health.'
>
> *Maimonidies (1135–1204), Jewish philosopher and Rabbinic scholar.*

▶ *In Pakistan, Muslim men meet and socialize in teahouses where they enjoy drinking tea, rather than alcohol.*

3. What does alcohol do?

How does alcohol make you act and feel?

Alcohol goes first to the stomach and is then carried round the whole body and into each organ, including the brain, by the bloodstream. After one or two drinks, a person will begin to feel happy, relaxed and carefree. As they continue to drink, they will begin to find it more difficult to do certain things, for example, to drive a car. The brain will no longer function properly, and it will become more difficult to remember things, to talk and even to walk properly.

If someone has had a lot to drink, people will say they are 'drunk'. If they continue drinking they will become very confused, collapse and could even die from alcohol poisoning.

'The first alcohol I tried was champagne and wine at my aunt's wedding. I only had one glass and it made me feel all woozy.'
Diana, aged 13.

◀ *After one or two drinks most people begin to feel more relaxed and carefree.*

▶ *Sometimes, after several drinks, people find themselves doing things which they would never normally do – such as singing loudly and shouting.*

THE SHORT-TERM EFFECTS OF DRINKING ALCOHOL

Blood alcohol (mg/100ml)	Beer drunk (pints)	The effects on your mind and body
20	$^1/_2$ - $^3/_4$	Judgement is affected, tension is released, feel more carefree.
50	$1^1/_2$	Tension and inhibitions of everyday life lessened. Driving performance affected.
60	2	Hand and arm movements affected, speech becomes clumsy. Driving affected badly.
80	$2^1/_2$ - 3	Begin to stagger, talk loudly, emotions are affected. Unsafe to drive.
100	3	Deeper areas of the brain affected, feel confused, may become sleepy.
160	5	May become aggressive. Memory loss is possible.
300	10	Difficult to arouse if asleep, not capable of voluntary action, equivalent to surgical anaesthesia. Could lose control of bodily functions.
500	18	Coma, anaesthesia of part of brain controlling breathing and heartbeat. Likely to die without medical assistance.

* This a rough guide to the effects of drinking. Other factors, such as age, weight and sex, determine an individual's reaction to alcohol.

What does alcohol do to your body?

Alcohol can cause long-term damage to the body if it is taken in large amounts regularly over months and years. However, a young drinker will not be damaged in the long term if they stop drinking or drink sensibly and follow guidelines for healthy drinking.

The whole of the body is affected by alcohol. These are the changes to the main organs which happen when a person drinks alcohol:

- heart – alcohol makes the heartbeat increase. This speeds up the rate at which blood travels around the body. In the long term, this might cause problems with circulation and blood pressure.
- liver – the liver breaks down and eliminates alcohol and other toxins from the body. This process takes time and the liver can only cope with 15 milligrams of alcohol every hour, which is nearly half a pint of beer or just less than one small glass of wine. In the long term, if someone drinks large amounts of alcohol every day, the liver never gets a break and will eventually become damaged.

◄ *After a night of heavy drinking you are likely to have a hangover the next day.*

◀ *These men are heavy drinkers. Many people who drink too much look older than they actually are.*

- stomach – drinking too much alcohol in the long term can cause ulcers which are painful and can stop a person from being able to eat properly.
- brain – the brain is affected by alcohol very quickly. How the brain is affected will depend on how much alcohol a person has had to drink and how quickly the alcohol reaches the brain. If a meal is eaten while drinking alcohol it takes longer for the alcohol to affect the brain. In the long term, drinking too much can cause sleeplessness, loss of memory and anxiety.

FACT:
Pregnant women who drink risk having babies with foetal alcohol defects. The most serious defects include mental problems, growth deficiency, head and facial deformities, joint and limb abnormalities, and heart defects.
Facts about Alcohol, Addiction Research Foundation, Toronto, Canada.

How much is it safe to drink?

Alcohol is measured in units. Each type of alcohol contains a certain number of units. For example, a standard glass of sherry contains one unit of alcohol. Half a pint of cider or a single shot of spirit also contain one unit.

Scientists are constantly studying how alcohol affects our health and how many units are safe for us to drink. Recent research found that small amounts, such as one to three units per day, of alcohol may protect a person against heart disease. Many people now drink some alcohol, especially red wine, each day for this reason. Other experts say that everyone should have at least one or two days each week which are alcohol-free.

But research can be misleading and some health experts insist that drinking alcohol causes social problems which are just as dangerous to our health. Violence after winning or losing at sport and violence in people's homes can be triggered by excessive drink. The important thing about drinking is knowing when to stop and knowing how much you as an individual can drink. Drinking alcohol is all about knowing yourself and your own limitations.

Alcohol and violence often go together. This fighting took place in May 2000 between Turkish and English football fans.

case study · case study · case study

Paul had his eighteenth birthday party coming up. He wanted to celebrate with his friends but knew his mum and dad would be worried about alcohol and everyone getting too drunk. They were scared that it would be like his older brother's party, when the police were called by neighbours. Paul decided to talk it through with his parents and come to some kind of compromise. His parents had gone away for his brother's party so they all decided it would be better if they were around for Paul's party. After talking it through they planned a family party with a DJ for the young people. They decided there would be some alcohol but also lots of food and non-alcoholic drinks.Paul was really happy with how the party went. Everybody had a good time and the police weren't called!

▼ *Many young men don't think they can have a good time without alcohol.*

How does alcohol affect different people?

> 'My first experience of really drinking alcohol was when my uncle brought a crate of beer to a party. I had five to six bottles. I didn't really have too many problems but I remember being very loud and people told me what embarrassing things I had said while drunk. I felt fine the next day. I think alcohol's an OK drug.'
> *Paul, 15.*
>
> 'Mine was worse than that. Last summer holidays we were at a party and I got so drunk that I climbed up onto the roof of a building. I lost my balance and ended up falling off – I really hurt myself. Then I was violently sick. I felt awful the next day. It's really put me off drink. I don't think alcohol is an OK drug.'
> *Marcus, 14.*

Alcohol is a very powerful drug and it affects one person completely differently from another. The effects depend on several factors:

- how much alcohol has been drunk in a given period of time
- how the drink is taken – whether it's mixed with other kinds of alcohol or with mixers
- the drinker's weight
- the drinker's height and sex
- how much food is in the stomach
- what kind of mood the person is in already

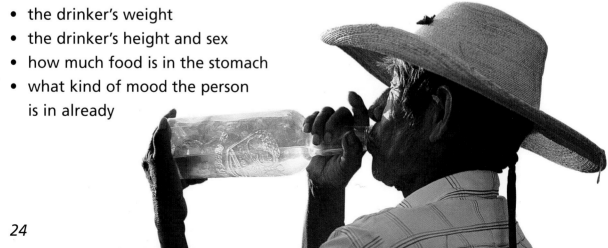

▼ *This man is used to drinking neat spirits. Most people would become very drunk if they tried to drink like this.*

- previous experience of drinking – how used to alcohol a person is already. People who drink regularly become used to the side-effects and can drink more before they suffer these bad effects
- current state of health

General guidelines for sensible drinking suggest that women should not drink more than 21 units of alcohol per week and that men should not drink more than 28 units of alcohol per week. Young people, who usually weigh less and are not as used to alcohol as most adults, should drink fewer units than the above guidelines for men and women.

▼ *Physically, women are less able to deal with alcohol, so the effects can be greater.*

4. Why do people drink alcohol?

The reasons people drink alcohol

People drink alcohol for many reasons but mostly because drinking helps them to enjoy themselves. It also helps people to relax and feel less shy. Many people think that the positive effects of drinking outweigh the negative effects.

> 'When I want to celebrate something really important, such as a birthday, I like champagne. At home, after work, I might have a glass of wine because I like the taste and because they say it's good for you!'
> *Lee, 27.*

▼ *World Champion Mika Hakkinen of Finland celebrates with champagne after the Spanish Formula One motor race in May 2000.*

Other reasons people drink alcohol include:

- to relax and relieve stress after a busy day
- to help people feel at ease when meeting new people
- what would a party be like without alcohol? Many people feel alcohol is necessary at a party to make sure everybody has a good time
- to celebrate anything from a wedding, a christening or a birthday, to winning at sport
- to complement food and cooking – as well as adding flavour to food, people like to drink alcohol with their meals. In some countries, such as France and Italy, it is traditional to drink wine with most meals
- for health reasons – some medical research shows that alcohol can be good for you
- it's easily available. In many countries take-away alcohol is sold in more and more outlets, such as supermarkets and convenience stores
- out of habit – alcohol can be addictive
- peer influence

▲ 'Cheers!' A toast with champagne to celebrate a twenty-first birthday party.

Young people and alcohol

Alcohol is a legal drug, which is used by many young people. It is easily available to under-age drinkers, because many of them look older than they really are and they can buy it from many take-away outlets. Most people also keep some alcohol at home, and this is where the majority of young people first experience alcohol. In this situation, either their parents give the alcohol to them, or they experiment with it secretly.

Other reasons young people decide to drink include:

- to get the buzz – alcohol can be exciting and fun
- to fit in with the crowd – peer influence
- to feel popular and less nervous in social situations
- to help to forget problems at home or school
- out of boredom – drinking alcohol is something to do at the weekend
- drinking seems more exciting and grown-up than other social activities such as sport or going to the cinema

▲ *Playing sport for some young people is a good way to keep fit and avoid the habit of drinking too much alcohol.*

One of the main reasons young people drink is because they think it shows they are grown-up. Boys may feel it makes them seem more like men. They think that drinking shows they are adults, while drinking large quantities and not getting drunk is macho. Girls may drink to show they can keep up with the boys. Research in many countries shows that young people are drinking earlier and drinking more.

FACT:
A new study shows that binge drinking on college campuses increased by 14% between 1993 and 1999... Binge drinking is defined as a man consuming five or more drinks in a row, or a woman having four or more consecutive drinks.
Journal of American College Health, 2000.

▼ *These French students have had a lot to drink. Some young people are tempted to drink too much because their friends are doing the same.*

Why do advertising and the media make people drink?

▲ *Pictures and images used in advertising often only show the glamorous side of drinking alcohol.*

Even though alcohol is a drug, it is, for most people, socially acceptable. As a result, alcohol regularly appears in the media. Films and television programmes frequently show people drinking alcohol and having fun. And, during the break, advertisements show similar exciting images.

FACT:
Research on responses to alcohol advertising on television showed that the more boys aged fourteen to seventeen liked the advertisements, the more likely they were to be drinkers, to have higher annual consumption (about 67 cans over the past year), and to expect to drink more frequently in the future.
Linda Hill, Young People and Alcohol, Child to Adult: The Dunedin Study.

case study · case study · case study · case study · case study

Paul always watched a lot of films and television. He particularly liked action films and there were always cool people drinking beer. 'It was always in my face, I just couldn't get away from it,' he said. Paul was eleven when he decided to try lager with a group of school friends. One night, when Paul's parents were out, they found a crate of lager in the garage and decided to drink it for a laugh. It was really good fun to start with – the beer didn't taste very nice but it made everyone giggle. They drank more and more and enjoyed dancing and messing about. Paul suddenly felt giddy though. He was sick on the carpet and passed out. The next morning he felt terrible and told himself he'd never drink again.

Some people argue that alcohol is as bad for people's health as cigarettes. However, tobacco advertising is banned while advertisements for alcohol are everywhere – on the television, in magazines and on billboards. Advertisers of alcohol know that most people think drinking alcohol is sophisticated and fun. They play upon this fact by producing advertisements which show attractive people enjoying alcohol in exotic locations or in exciting situations. Some advertisements are specially targeted at younger people.

▶ *Some movies seem to glamorize drinking alcohol. In the film* Cocktail, *Tom Cruise plays a hip young barman.*

5. What are the problems with alcohol?

How does alcohol affect society?

Most people do not have problems with alcohol. However, as the number of people who drink rises, the problems associated with alcohol increase too.

Drinking and driving is one of the worst alcohol-related problems. Young drivers who drink are five times more likely to have an accident than non-drinkers. Many parents are concerned about the levels of drinking and driving amongst adults, as well as among young people. In the USA, a Californian mother, whose thirteen-year-old daughter was killed by a drunken driver in 1980, started the organization called MADD (Mothers against Drunk Driving). The organization campaigns for stricter laws against drinking and driving and has 3 million members in the USA.

▶ *The risk of a car accident is higher when a person has been drinking.*

An anti-drinking sign painted by children in Sri Lanka is a sad reminder of the problems with alcohol.

Every year, all over the world, many work days are lost due to people being off sick with hangovers or other alcohol-related problems – this results in a loss of profit to many businesses.

The cost to hospitals and health services for alcohol-related illnesses is also increasing. Alcohol not only causes physical health problems, it can cause mental health problems, such as depression and, possibly, suicide.

There is also a growing number of crimes which are directly related to the use and abuse of alcohol. Violent crime, especially domestic violence and child abuse, while under the influence of alcohol is on the increase.

> 'The majority of our patients come in with problems that are related to alcohol in some way or another. You have fights, car crashes and accidents and then there is the illness, all of which are caused by too much alcohol over many years. Personally, I feel it is a very dangerous drug in every way.'
> *Nurse, UK.*

What is alcohol dependency?

It is important to remember that alcohol is a drug and, as with any other drug, one of the dangers is dependency or addiction. Some people become physically dependent on alcohol which means that their bodies do not work properly without drinking alcohol and they feel sick if they do not drink alcohol.

FACT:
Many famous people have been drink-dependent or had parents who were dependent on alcohol. Ludwig van Beethoven (1770-1827), the famous German composer, had a drink-dependent father. As a result, Beethoven had to go out to work at an early age. He managed to support his family as a singer in the court chapel. Elvis Presley (1935-1977), the singer and actor, died aged just forty-two of what is thought to have been drug and alcohol abuse.

◀ *Elvis Presley in 1971, just six years before he died. At the height of his success Elvis had been a sex symbol, but here he is starting to look ill from years of alcohol and drug abuse.*

Many people can drink alcohol in moderation but others cannot control the amount they drink and alcohol begins to take over their lives. They don't drink for pleasure; they drink because they cannot do without alcohol.

We sometimes assume that people who are dependent on alcohol are loners or homeless. But many drinkers have good jobs with a home and family to support. These people find it difficult to admit they have a problem with alcohol. They may not seem to get particularly drunk when they drink but they need to drink to cope with their lives.

▼ *Alcohol dependency can mean drinking anything with alcohol in it. These South Africans drink a deadly mixture of beer and car battery fluid.*

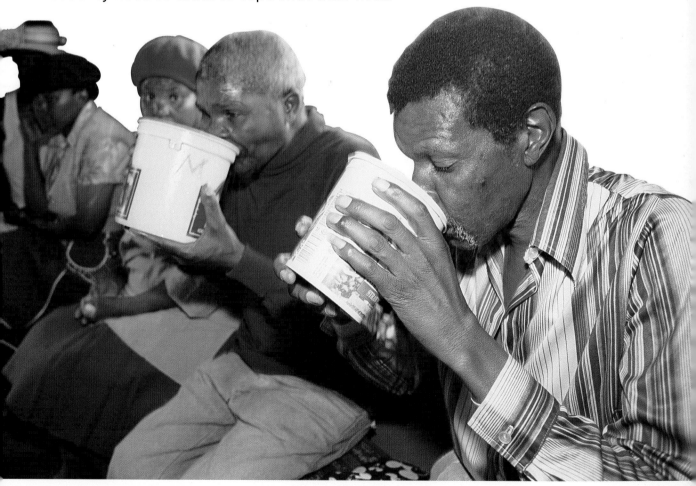

How do people become drink-dependent?

There are many different reasons why someone becomes drink-dependent. It is not easy to say exactly why one person becomes drink-dependent and another does not. Some people do not cope well with stress and have a particularly difficult home or work life. Perhaps something has happened in a person's life to make them depressed or lonely, or they may be poor, or have a personality problem. Some people start drinking out of boredom but then drink out of habit and use drink to cope with life.

> FACT:
> Those children who had tried alcohol at age nine were more likely than others to have experienced alcohol-related problems by age eighteen.
> *Linda Hill, Young People and Alcohol.*

◀ *Losing a husband or wife can be one of the many reasons somebody starts to drink heavily.*

case study · case study · case study · case study · case study

Sarah was a friend of Gail's for many years. Gail had noticed at times that Sarah's behaviour was strange, secretive and, once or twice, she had even lied about certain things. Gail never for one minute thought that Sarah was an alcoholic. Sarah was a nurse and held a very responsible position in the hospital where she worked. She was a kind and thoughtful person and her patients thought the world of her. Then, one day, Sarah admitted herself to a special unit for treating people with alcohol problems. She told Gail she had been drinking heavily since she was fourteen years old.

A person does not become alcohol-dependent overnight. It usually takes several years for alcohol dependency to develop. Some people drink heavily for many years without actually realizing that they are dependent on alcohol.

With the increasing number of teenagers starting to drink at a younger and younger age, governments around the world are concerned that there will be a rise in the number of young people who are dependent on alcohol over the next few years.

▶ *When the pressures of work and family life get too much, alcohol can seem the answer for some people.*

Where can people with problems get help?

The most important first step for someone with alcohol dependency is for them to admit that they have a problem and that they need help. Even then the road to recovery will not be easy, but unless they acknowledge that they have a problem with alcohol, they cannot start to get better.

Treatment for people with alcohol problems can be in hospitals or special units, or at support meetings and counselling groups. The process of giving up alcohol or 'drying out' is a long and difficult one. The person may need to receive medication to help deal with the painful withdrawal symptoms. They might need treatment for other conditions, such as liver or stomach problems, caused by years of heavy drinking.

▼ *Counselling is an important part of recovering from alcohol dependency.*

'I drank just to get rid of my feeling of not being wanted or really loved. It took me a broken marriage and nearly losing my job before I would admit that I needed help.'
Shaun, aged 40, who started drinking at the age of 12.

Many people who are dependent on alcohol need to learn to live without drinking ever again – this is called living in sobriety. Some people continue to drink in moderation but this is difficult because they have an addiction. Many recovering dependent drinkers join an organization called Alcoholics Anonymous (AA). The organization provides people with the help and support of other recovering drinkers or ex-drinkers.

There are other organizations which can provide help for the families of dependent drinkers. These groups help the families to support the recovering dependent drinker.

Many people believe that once someone is dependent on alcohol they are dependent for life. It is not easy to recover from being a dependent drinker but many people, with the help of organizations like the AA, can overcome their dependency.

▶ *Help can be just a phone call away but admitting there is a problem has to come first.*

6. Making choices about alcohol

What do different people think about alcohol?

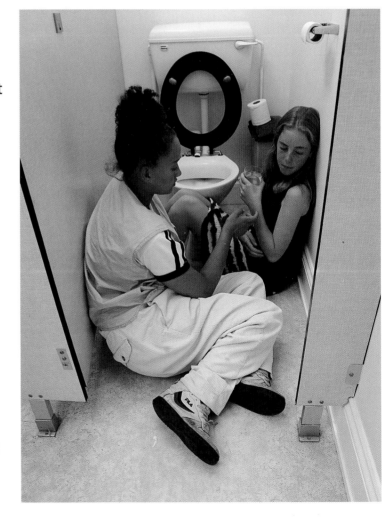

▼ *Drinking alcohol isn't always fun – this girl has just been sick and needs her friend's help.*

People have many different thoughts and feelings about alcohol. Their opinion depends on their own personal experience. Perhaps someone has an alcoholic in their family and they have seen the damage that alcohol can do to the whole family. If someone works as a nurse or ambulance driver, they see sick and injured people every day whose problems are caused by alcohol.

A young person who gets drunk for the first time and has fun might think drinking alcohol is exciting. A young person who gets drunk for the first time and is sick would probably have a very different opinion.

40

Everyone has their own thoughts about drinking alcohol. Listen to these different voices:

'A lot of the time with our work, alcohol has been involved in some way or another. I drink, but having seen all the problems that are caused by alcohol, I drink in moderation.'
Ambulance driver, New York, USA.

'Friday and Saturday night fights are triggered by people just not knowing when to stop drinking. This leads to arguments which end up in a big fight. This isn't just in the pubs and clubs but also in people's homes.'
Policeman, Birmingham, UK.

'It's OK if you drink a little bit of alcohol and become merry. But if you drink a lot and become drunk it is not very nice for people around you.'
Julian, 13, Lille, France.

'Come off it! A party with no booze? You've got to be joking.'
Michael, 21, Manchester, UK.

'I like my glass of wine after a long day at work.'
Janette, 31, Illinois, USA.

▶ *Many people can enjoy a drink without becoming alcoholic.*

Making choices about alcohol

Alcohol use among young people is rising. As we have seen, young people's ability to manage alcohol is not as effective as that of adults, but it can be done.

You all have choices to make when it comes to alcohol:

- you decide whether you want to drink or not
- you are in control of the amount you drink
- you can encourage your friends to drink or you can respect their choices
- you know when you're over the limit and can say 'no' at any time

▲ *If you do drink alcohol, then only you can decide how much is right for you to drink.*

case study · case study · case study · case study · case study

When Kathy was fifteen she saw alcohol as a rite of passage to growing up. If she could show everyone how much she could drink and that she could handle her drink then her mates would look up to her. One day she made a bet with Jo, her best friend. They bet on who could drink the most. That was when it all went horribly wrong. They started drinking some lager and then, when they ran out, they stole vodka from Kathy's parents' drink cabinet. Both girls drank until they passed out. Fortunately, Kathy's mother found them and called an ambulance. They both ended up in hospital with alcohol poisoning.

FACT:

A survey of young people aged fifteen to sixteen found that many young people experience problems due to the misuse of alcohol. On average, 21% of teenagers reported individual problems, such as reduced performance at school. 22% reported relationship problems, 15% reported sexual problems, such as unwanted or unprotected sex, and 12% reported delinquency problems, such as violence and fighting.

1995 ESPAD Report, CAN and Council of Europe, 1997.

Remember:
- 1 glass of wine   =   1 unit
- 1/2 pint of beer/lager   =   1 unit
- 1 can of strong lager   =   3 units
- 1/2 bottle of vodka   =   15 units
- 1 glass of a soft drink   =   0 units

What choices will you make when it comes to alcohol?

▼ *After working all week, these young Zambian men enjoy a few beers on a Friday night – it's their way of relaxing.*

Taking care with alcohol

Alcohol is part of our society. Even though it is a dangerous drug and causes many problems in society it is still legal. But it is possible to drink sensibly and carefully, and have a good time.

Tips for sensible drinking:

- always have food with alcohol – alcohol drunk on an empty stomach is absorbed quickly into the body
- alternate non-alcoholic drinks with alcoholic drinks
- think about what you are drinking – generally the higher the alcohol content of the drink, the more quickly it is absorbed into your body. Vodka, for example, is absorbed faster than beer
- do not mix your drinks – for example, wine and spirits shouldn't be mixed
- beware of spirits mixed with a soft drink – vodka and lemonade might not taste as strong as neat vodka but it still has lots of vodka in it
- try to drink only at weekends or on special occasions
- plan how much you are going to drink before you go out with your friends and stick to your plan

▼ *Drinking orange juice between each alcoholic drink is this girl's way of taking care she doesn't get too drunk – what will you do?*

- if someone says they do not want another drink, do not pressurize them into having one
- if someone tries to pressurize you into having another drink, and you don't want another, say 'No!' – you are your own person, and you can stand up for yourself

Alcohol is part of our society and it is here to stay. It can be used safely, and in a fun way, without harming your health – it's up to you.

▲ *Drinking alcohol is just one way of having fun. Lots of young people find other things which give them a buzz.*

'One thing I know about alcohol is that it can be very dangerous and that it is not good to drink too much of it. You can become addicted to it and it can make you do things you do not want to do and it can influence your mind. It is OK to have a little bit of alcohol but not too much.'
Katy, 11.

GLOSSARY

Addiction
When a person cannot stop doing something, even when it is harmful.

Alcoholic
A person who is addicted to drinking alcohol.

Binge drinking
When a person drinks one alcoholic drink after another, very quickly.

Breweries
Buildings where beer or lager is usually produced.

Consumption
The purchase and use of something, i.e. alcohol.

Delinquency
Minor crimes, usually committed by young people.

Dependency
When a person has to have something to help them cope with life.

Depressant drug
A drug which causes the body to slow down. Alcohol is a depressant drug.

Distillation
The process of evaporating or boiling a liquid to make it more concentrated or purer.

Domestic violence
When a person hits out at and hurts the person they are married to or live with.

Drying out
When somebody who drinks too much stops drinking.

Fermentation
A chemical reaction in which yeast breaks down the sugar in fruit, for example, and changes it to alcohol.

Growth deficiency
When a baby or child fails to grow properly. This can happen as a baby is forming in the mother's womb.

Hangover
The after-effects of drinking too much alcohol. Effects include headache, tiredness and sickness.

Intoxicating
Something, such as alcohol, which makes a person drunk or over-excited.

Legal
When something is allowed by law.

Licence
Permission from an authority to allow pubs, restaurants, wine bars, etc., to sell alcohol.

Licensed premises
A place where alcohol is allowed to be sold.

Long term
Something which goes on for a long time.

Macho
When sombody does something to make themselves look big and cool. Usually used to describe boys and men.

Measure
A certain quantity or amount of any substance.

Minimum legal age
The youngest age at which you are allowed to do something by law.

Moderate drinking
Drinking amounts of alcohol which do not exceed the recommended weekly amounts, i.e. 21 units for women and 28 units for men.

Peer influence
When a person feels pressurized to do something because everyone else is doing it.

Prohibit
To stop something from happening.

Short term
Something which happens for a short time.

Sobriety
When a person does not get drunk from alcohol. We often say that a person lives in sobriety.

Teetotal
Used to describe a person who does not drink any alcohol.

Under-age drinking
Drinking alcohol below the legal age for drinking.

FURTHER INFORMATION

ORGANIZATIONS

Worldwide there are organizations providing information and advice about alcohol. The organizations below can supply educational material and resources. Information is also available on the Internet.

UK

Alcoholics Anonymous
PO BOX 1
Stonebow House
Stonebow
York
YO1 2NJ
Tel: 01904 644 026
(local helpline numbers are available in all local telephone directories)

Alcohol Concern
Waterbridge House
32–36 Loman Street
London
SE1 0EE
Tel: 020 7928 7377
http://www.alcoholconcern.org.uk

Al-anon Family Groups
24-hour helpline for families and friends of problem drinkers.
Tel: 020 7403 0888

Drinkline
Gives confidential support and advice. Will put you in touch with your local alcohol advice centre.
Tel: 0345 32 02 02

Health Education Authority
Hamilton House
Mabledon Place
London
WC1H 9TX
Tel: 020 741 1888
http://www.hea.org.uk

National Drugs Helpline
Tel: 0800 77 66 00

TACADE (Teacher's Advisory Council on Alcohol and Drug Education)
1 Hulme Place
The Crescent
Salford
Greater Manchester
N5 4QA
Tel: 0161 745 8925

USA

Alcoholics Anonymous
PO Box 459
Grand Central Station
New York, 10163
Tel: (212) 870 3400

NCADD (National Council on Alcoholism and Drug Dependence)
12 West 21 Street
New York 10010
Tel: (212) 206 6770
http://www.ncadd.org

FURTHER READING

Books for children
A Young Person's Guide to Alcohol by Stephen Roos (Hazelden Educational, 1993)
Learn to say no: Alcohol (Heinemann, 2000)
We're Talking about Alcohol by Jenny Bryan (Hodder Wayland, 1995)
What do you Know about Drinking? by Pete Sanders (Franklin Watts)

Books for adults
Alcohol by Terry Brown (Folens, 1999)
Alcohol by Pavla and Paula McGuire (Raintree/Steck Vaughn, 1998)
Alcohol and You (Impact Series) by Jane Claypool (Franklin Watts, 1997)
Dr. Miriam Stoppard's Drug Information File: From Alcohol and Tobacco to Ecstasy and Heroin (Dorling Kindersley, 1999)
Let's Talk About Alcohol Abuse by Marianne Johnston (Rosen Publishing Group, 1997)

INDEX